Praise for David Dephy

A Literature Luminary / **Bowery Poetry**
The Incomparable Poet / **Statorec**
The Stellar Poet / **Voices of Poetry**
Brilliant Grace / **Headline Poetry and Press**
What a lovely prayer! / **Life and Legends Magazine**
An Extremally Unique Poetic Voice / **Cultural Daily**
So great ~*Laurie Anderson*

These poems are filled with life—not just any life, but deeply energetic, optimistic, and determined energy. Reading through these pages has been the most vivifying experience I've had in a long time. ~ ***DW Gibson,*** The New York Times columnist, an American award-winning writer & journalist.

Reading after David Dephy is like playing after Jimi Hendrix when Jimi finished his set. ~***Aaron Fischer,*** *National Award-Winning Poet.*

David Dephy doesn't just write poetry, he is poetry. ~***Lucas Hirsch****, International Award-Winning Dutch Poet and Novelist.*

This work is light, and shadows whispered in breaths of silent beauty, in words that bridge the distance between hatred, war in Ukraine and in Georgia, and love, in the voice of nature to carry the reader in caring hands on a splendid journey to face truth. Dephy is a poetry master of the melody of questions that yearn for answers, that display our quest for knowledge in sacred verse; he holds back nothing in connecting fear and loss to wanting and waiting patient for shadows to birth light in a golden dawn. These poems beg for forgiveness, for an understanding of war and bombings; they embrace an intrinsic love of New York and all its stories of laughter and pain. This is a must-read collection, one you will thumb through and read again many times in your own search for truths. Take the hand David offers, become like air as time becomes endless. ~ *J R Turek, New York Poet of the Year, Editor, Workshop Leader.*

David Dephy's work is an intense and moving exploration of the aftermath of historical violence. Having lived through the 2008 Russian invasion of Georgia, and having arrived in the US ten years later, Dephy expresses a Whitmanian faith in America's highest ideals and, at the same time, a determination to reach inwardly toward love and a productive peacefulness. Dephy's view of the world is expansive and elemental, full of shadow and light, fear, and hope. To look up and find "no fighter aircraft . . . but kites," to decide that "the only true protest is beauty"—these are how we inhabit the freedom of the moment, Dephy tells us, as he points us repeatedly toward our better selves with his strong poetic voice. ~*Wayne Miller*, *National Award-Winning Poet. An Author of We the Jury. Professor, English Department Chair the University of Colorado, Denver, the Editor of Copper Nickel.*

In this work David Dephy is not just a superb lyrical poet of tender moments, not just a documentarian of sociopolitical crises or a new-romantic lover sharing the grief of loss, his writing is philosophical and mystical, suffused with love of humanity and exhortations to us to dwell in, and delve more deeply into, the spiritual and ephemeral, to be transformative in our vision of ourselves as individuals and as a society. He tells us early in his book that "we all are alone in our own journey / but many are going with us," reminding us of the paradoxes that mark our lives – simple and complex, tragic, and sublime, lonely and supported— and that we are all one, all connected. Dephy declares: "...there is one endless music in the world / and all these songs .../ all these melodies /... are just the parts / of its enormous body...." This important poetry collection affirms the need for us to seek truth and beauty; for us to be humble in the presence of nature, which Dephy personifies elegantly, exposing the wisdom of trees, leaves, rivers, bridges, cities, bees, deadly sound of bombs, aircraft, death and of course hope teaching us truths; and for us to fully realize that love is everything, that only love is real, and love always wins. ~*Thelma T. Reyna, National Award-Winning Poet, Ph.D., the University of California, the Author of Dearest Papa: A Memoir in Poems, the Editor of Golden Foothills Poetry Anthology.*

When I first saw David Dephy read his poem at the Bowery Poetry in Manhattan I thought of William Blake. It was an instinctive response, rather than critical or intellectual, born of the poem's aphoristic intelligence, its refusal to reduce the world to the commonplace. That same engagement shimmers through this book. ~ *Aaron Fischer, An American Award-Winning Poet. An Author of Black Stars of Blood: The Weegee Poems.*

David Dephy surely carries the spirit of America in his heart and adeptly builds up the poetry perception. We find his works to be extremely unique and attractive. David Dephy's poetic voice is strong, his poetic world is extraordinarily rich. *~**Linda Galbraith** for **Cultural Daily***

We deeply admired David Dephy's works. We enjoyed how he used nature to portray complex emotions, and we loved the intertwining of natural occurrences and human experiences. The parallels were really haunting, and we loved it. *~**McKenzie Lynn Tozan** / An Editor of Lit Shark and American Essayist and Poet.*

The way the David's poem cuts fantasy with reality and highlights the relief of arriving is beautifully done. It truly pushes the boundaries of art, humanity, and beauty. **~Pena Literary Magazine**

Profound, understated, conclusive, rhythmic, repetitive. A maestro at work! **~Fevers of the Mind Magazine**

David Dephy's mesmerizing talent captivates listeners, hypnotizes everyone in the hall, drawing them into a whirlwind of emotion.
~Poetry Forum

His poetry is about the profound impact of living in war-torn times. The disillusionment with authority figures and the haunting remnants of past conflicts. As people navigate a landscape filled with forgotten and misplaced memories, they find themselves haunted by the dreams and unresolved issues of those who came before them. In a world scarred by past wars, how do we navigate the path to peace and understanding? David Dephy captures the essence of these turbulent times with his evocative language. His work often addresses themes of history, identity, and the human condition. **~Litehouse**

Rays Never Were
So Near As Now

Rays Never Were So Near As Now

Collected Poems
2020–2024

David Dephy

WESTBRAE LITERARY GROUP

ISBN: 979-8-9917199-2-6
Published by Westbrae Literary Group
Berkeley, California
Jon-David Hague, Founding Editor

For more information about this and other titles from Westbrae Literary Group, visit us at westbraeliterarygroup.com or email us at info@westbraeliterarygroup.com

For my wife Kethy and our sons Gega, Andro, and Deme who made me put a light in and showed me that distance means nothing when your loved ones mean everything.

~ D. D.

CONTENTS

Chapter One
The Convex Function of Parallel Ray

The Gift...20

D Train..21

Streets...22

Roses..23

Behind Every Droplet...24

Hope..25

Time Square 26

Before Dawn..27

If I Said a Word..28

The Heart of a Cyclone..29

Time is Up..30

Forest..31

For a Second..32

Heaven Hear Us..34

A Bird Above New York City.................................35

Chapter Two
The Definition of Focal Ray

Fog..38

The Sky..40

Jerusalem...41

The Flow of the Current......................................42

The Sky Is Clear Tonight...................................43

Herald Square Was Drifting That Night..........45

A Few Centuries Pass.......................................47

Take Your Sandals Off Your Feet....................48

In The Dark..49

Forever for One Second...................................50

Through Our Wishes..51

R Train..54

A Cloud...55

A Wave..56

By Our Presence...57

Chapter Three
The Structure of Central Ray

Empty Space..60

Divine Drunkenness..61

Statue of Liberty..62

Love Song of Rays...63

As The Breath of Mother.................................65

Lattice Weave..54

96-Year-Old Man...66

All the Shores of Mediterranean Sea.................68

With a Million Smiles..70

Let It Stand..71

Remember Me..72

Empty Strollers in Front of You..........................73
Divine Ukraine...74
The Mirrors...75
Wolf Came to Me, Once.....................................76
If I Spoke the Tongues of Men..........................77
Acknowledgements...81

The Three Rays concept typically refers to the three principal rays used to construct ray diagrams for lenses and mirrors, which are: the parallel ray, the focal ray, and the central ray; where the parallel ray travels parallel to the principal axis, the focal ray passes through the focal point, and the central ray goes through the center of the lens or mirror without deviation. The Three Rays are fundamentally important in visionary world and fundamentally are the same: a parallel ray that bounces through the focal point, a focal ray towards the focal point that bounces parallel, and a central ray going right through the center of the lens and mirrors. Here are the key points about these rays:

The Convex Function of Parallel Ray

When drawn, it will refract or reflect and pass through the focal point of the lens or mirror. The parallel ray travels parallel to the principal axis.

The Definition of Focal Ray

When drawn, it will refract or reflect and become parallel to the principal axis. The focal ray passes through the focal point.

The Structure of Central Ray

This ray passes through the center of the lens or mirror and continues the same path without bending. The central ray goes through the center of the lens or mirror without deviation.

Chapter One

The Convex Function of Parallel Ray

The Gift

In my childhood
I have had an ability
of saying words
in a very different way.

If I was saying "Rose,"
people were feeling
the smell of the rose,
immediately,

by saying "Coffee"
people were feeling
the smell of fresh hot coffee.
I lost that gift when I grew up,

but I found it once again
when I was miserable,
left alone, left for dead.
I said: "Hope,"

and you appeared,
sitting right next to me
in the empty subway station
waiting for a train.

D Train

D train, moves from Brooklyn to Manhattan
and back, there is always something to be made
of loneliness, it's obvious you feel the same,
we hear the strange sound of heartbeat — music,
you hear the same sound, of the same heartbeat,
and maybe someone turns out pain in every sound
of train? They kept your smile while the D train

rushed over and over, taking us along, between
those golden shadows all around, solitude unites,
it breaks free, hear me, please, hear me out from
this noise, it is heroic to survive as breath buried
in the claustrophobic darkness, take a D train, baby,
wherever you go take a deep breath, the way is long,
moving to the garden we all go through the desert, first.

Streets

Looking at the empty streets.
Beauty needs to be seen.
I know you are happy out there
on the other side of emptiness,
yet the present is the choice
which remains. In admiration,
beauty, in poverty wealth
and in silence the sound,
I will put the gun down,
who stands beside me matters more.
I'll remember this second,
on the other side of what was emptiness,
I'll remember this present, but the streets
will be alive again, only that which needs
to be seen will be.

Roses

Roses have a smell of mysteries,
requiring some courage in your hands.
Can you hear that noise from the other side?
The noise of wheels, and screams,
that's how the void swallows the world,
you run and you try to catch that smell,
but you don't feel the ground under your feet,
you only feel the hot steam of blood,
leaving the misty burrs behind,
surrounded with the prickle fur and gorged gardens,
and fields spewing infinite echoes of distant bells.
Roses have a smell of peace, nothing beside remains,
round the decay of nightmares, boundless and bare,
the lone echoes of laughter and bells stretch far away.

Behind Every Droplet

Waiting for the news we are divided.
Spinning chaos into order,
still living without a sense
of what's buried deep
within the night.

Perhaps, behind every droplet
is a microcosm of purest energy
and behind that force, a window
of hope, and behind each window
a smile, and behind the ringing
of laughter, a tender kiss—
for is not beyond each kiss
a breath which is the throbbing
heart of life? — and there, right
there beneath the rib cage,
a wish, and deeper still,
that lingering desire
for a moment realized,
and beyond, further beyond,
the great flame
which is eternity rekindled
endlessly, until we begin
to believe we may be.

Hope

Listening to your voice
on the other side of silence
gives me the courage
to lose sight and swim there,
your voice is hope trusting the flow.
It calls me now:
we are what we hear,
doubt is deadlier,
but fear cuts
deeper than air,
and I am not moving toward revenge,
I forgive myself my own loneliness.
It's hard to form.

Time Square

Time has spirit,
through the incarnation the spirit of time
became fully human and fully divine,
these natures cannot be separated.
Still entwined, we all are alone
in our own journey
but many are going with us,
and time passes as time does,
so much behind us, a little less to go.
No easy ride, peace can be vexing—
what we've left behind us
the sun deeps down low,
and the way out of past is through now, only,
and we miss nothing,
we reached for the secret right on time,
and when the moon rose over Manhattan,
we felt our existence, it meant time was endless,
and its portals, as breathe between chasms,
opened and closed, and rearranged the wings
on our shoulders — constellations,
and clustered the words all around—
the seeds of silence fell in dark drifts.

Before Dawn

A stillness broken
before dawn,

in the name of
all that's hailed,

in the name of
our very present,

in the face of it all—
the remaining past

unclaimed, driven
forth by faith.

If I Say a Word

In that night, when the moon rose over the bridge,
and the shores divided, we've come too close together
toward the very beginning of desperation.

We had no reason to talk, we were alone, but now—
will talking disturb you if I say a word? Any word.
Yet, the noise has gone, and the room is finally empty,

no thoughts, no memories, no sound and no furry,
and no winter of our discontent, no questions anymore,
the afternoons in this room have grown quiet again,

as the days of our youth, and warm again, encircled by rays.
We knew what the beginning meant, but these nights,
we are no longer even certain, is there a hope in our hearts,

that war could be avoided? Or something to be made of joy?
How could it exist, when all those years we stored our
golden
hearts as though the loneliness was gone forever.

The Heart of a Cyclone

Each tree, the heart
of a wind. Each wind
a string on time's lyre:

divine love reflected
upon its own reflection,
wickedness kindling

that flame of darkness,
but when the hero strikes
her anvil of freedom,

the vision returns: here
the mist is a single thought
floating within islands of silence.

Time Is Up

Night tells us who's most precious,
most close—
which reflection most resembles our hearts.

Night has a heart of a prophet.

When we were young and went to that garden,
we saw the silkworm, but time is up,
it is a butterfly now.

Forest

Sick of the illusions raised by the killers,
became teachers.

Sick of the dust raised by those teachers,
became fools.

On the edge of the past, the fears are rolling over.
We are still running all around each other

in forest and its dark stillness. A stillness never tells
the truth. Forest is only a body of leaf's soul.

We still believe the war is over now, but do not recall
who won it. Kind people, no doubt, for only they

would leave so many dead. Their last breath
keeps us turning back to something forgotten,

to something misplaced, keeps us turning
back toward their dreams, which are blameless.

For a Second

For a second,
just for a second
on this silent afternoon,
I stopped the stream of
ugliness with my breath
and with my intention.

There was no death from
heaven anymore—
there were no falling
bombs, only the kites
and the valley under
the sun and my father's
voice was coming from
beyond the valley:
"Believe my boy, believe
my son," for a second
everything hushed so
quietly around me—
the same silence again

the same calmness again
hung above me and today
is like yesterday—

Everything, everything is
exactly the same, just like
yesterday, but without you.

Heaven Hear Us

You still hear the falling bombs
our Father in Heaven, to You do we sing
blessed and banished children of dust,
please rejoice with us, we love our enemies,
as we never loved them before, and still,
they are killing us, as they did before.
To you do we cry Mary, Mother of God,
please be a mother to us all now,
as we flit between the faded shadows
in our last afternoon.

A Bird Above New York City

The sky is getting closer with every breath.
I found everything when I found myself.
I am enough to the world.

The winds are running air, reside earth,
each in its own way, they are beauty of the world,
they are enough as they are.

I flew away from the nest directly to your heart, air,
you are enough — my mother sky, and I am getting
closer to you and closer,

into your arms I feel myself naked and free.
I feel strange when I look up to the sky.
Above me is a golden silence of my own expectations.

Maybe this man thinks he also can fly, maybe that one
tree knows the truth about all the locations of the oldest
treasures buried deep in the ground, and I am still looking

up to the sky where the seagull is chasing the breeze and
laughingly cries, when the morning relieves,
silently reveals all the mysteries of the night
when constellations were high.

Chapter Two

The Definition of Focal Ray

Fog

Fog lies low over the land.
Rain drives soft across the fields.
Comatose landscape.

There is nothing immediate we can hope for,
now we have nothing to do but breathe,
until something better shows up.

We are holding each other,
expecting a miracle at dawn,
as if there were no one and nothing to hurt us.

Beginning in mid-March the nights draw in,
our look turns warm and soft,
the fog passes gently over us,

we'd like to ask the fog—
don't talk to us, our heart's been broken,
we can't listen to you, we can't see you,

but the fog covers us and says:
I never see myself either,
in my own mind I'm invisible,

that's why you may feel I'm almighty,

you are like birds, your flight
begins and ends in silence,

you will find yourselves in each other only,
silence is garden, among the growing dreams
and precious wishes

you will discover each other again,
everything that will ever be discovered,
already exists in the mist.

The Sky

The sky grew within my heart, one day,
I was standing in the front yard.
The sky was so high it penetrated me through.
Oh, what a sky it was, so familiar and powerful
the memories as the leaves fell off the trees.
They were on the ground, as the imprints of glances
once when we saw each other for a very first time.
No fighter aircraft up there, but kites.

Jerusalem

Time is invisible at night—
the sound of premonition echoes in the dark,
thousand years ahead of eclipse,
and every night we give ourselves,
as if we found something precious
that it overwhelms all our wishes.

That star drifts above the black smoke.
Our loneliness is fading away.
The answer dwells in flickering flames
beyond the waters, mists, and dust,
showing us the meaning of trust,
expecting a miracle at dawn,
and we, reading the lines of lights
through the centuries of mysteries,
want to feel each other again,
we'd like to taste this second—
time of a miracle when truth emerges
in between echoes of explosions,
on the other side of alone.

The Flow of the Current

You need to go, I know, I see, the rivers are in you,
and oceans, and mountains, and heavens are in you,
and no one knows the trout that swim upstream

in those rivers. Trout must swim upstream to breathe.
Water enters their mouths, and exits the gills
as they face upstream, by facing upstream,

the trout catch whatever food comes their way
by the flow of the current, and not only food,
but dreams as well secretly told to water

by the pilgrims and saints, and no one knows how
their hearts are entwined rays the road carries
through the rapid circle of days and nights

toward us all. You will give them a key, today,
and will show them your door. You will walk with them,
today,
and will tell a story, not revealing the end of that story

until you speak in their tongue, until you care about them.
The sound of flow attracts you more and you need to go,
I see, trout must swim upstream.

The Sky Is Clear Tonight

Silence tomorrow,
the sky is clear tonight. See?
Still, the song echoes,
you know a song enough
to drown the notes

in silence as the seeds.
Mirages of clear water
across dusty horizons,
ripe expectations just
over the rise, right there.

An old photograph
makes us chuckle,
but now your smile
has such a glare,
I just can't tell.

This endless journey
keeps me turning back
to something forgotten,
to something misplaced,
keeps me turning back

toward you,
and the clouds above you
form as the moon rises,
and we still try to give them
a sense of purpose.

Herald Square was Drifting that Night

"I should find her, otherwise,
nothing makes sense," he thought
and jumped from the taxi on 34th Street,
at the intersection of Broadway,
Sixth Avenue.

Herald Square was drifting on the shadows
that night, he looked around to find any sign
of her left by the cold breeze of desperation,
"Is it all really over?" he though. "Where is
she?" the lava of separation encircled him,

the stream of people across the square,
enlightened with hope and wonder,
jeweled by the precious smiles
of expectations was clinging
to him, the street seemed endless,

he took a deep breath, closed his eyes,
noise had penetrated him, turning his prayer
into the sirens, he remembered sunlight,
flashing on her face, the fear of isolation
followed that noise, cutting his memories,

that was the last moment he remembered,
as if the cacophony of a century bore her
away, the chilling insight that from this

moment he couldn't live without her,
knowing that one who disappears from

the present always returns in the past.
It sounded wrong to him, nothing like
what he felt, but that noise sounded
conventional not so easy to accept.
He got love of holding, but now, he got

love of letting go for the very first time.
"Was it real?" he thought. "Or was it
the face of fate?" He knew something
was coming, something needed to happen,
the seeds grow slowly, but never remain

alone. "If she ran away," he thought. "Let her
be free, those who love you will take you
with them." He accepted the sound of sirens,
he breathed out, exiled the sky, realizing that
he was lost, finally. He was scared, alone.

"Are you OK?" he heard her voice and
opened his eyes. She was standing right
in front of him, softly confused in that
blue night. "What's the matter?" she spoke.
"Why are you looking at me like that?"

A Few Centuries Pass

The storms displace the world
without washing us away.
A few centuries pass.
The air fills with the same sound,
with the same smell and memories,
love of our life. In the front yard
we see some familiar faces, again,
and the lilac is studded with rays.
The world is lost, but we are young again.
We try to win our life back,
we say thank you past for lessons—
we are ready, that is the point of breathing,
many have gone forever, as in old news,
saying a few messages
we don't remember.

Take Your Sandals Off Your Feet

You are in Ukraine, take off your sandals,
for the place where you are standing
is holy and the air you are breathing is holy,
touching rays on your face,
drifting through the noise of madness
from the other side of the dark,
still, the lips touch the air
and this body is a foreign language
addressing a foreign world,
and its foreign skies. I say,
take a deep breath, my love,
let us embrace this great void as an old friend,
perhaps then we shall discover each other
far on the other side of alone.
Have you heard a song of braves?
Take your sandals off your feet,
the place where you're standing is holy,
every grain is the heart of a child,
the grain of truth—
breathing through the golden shadows.
Have you heard the laughs and smells?
This is the greatest afternoon of freedom.

In the Dark

Who says the hunt has begun?
Thank the Lord I stayed awake.
I thought of freedom running in the dark
with no difference of pits and graves,
when the mist of night was my only ally,
a man cannot be destroyed once and for all.
Now I feel the dawn is due to come,
right from your heart, from other side of alone.
I thought of you, how you took a deep breath
and said my name, how you exhaled the sky
from you with every letter of that name,
showing me the meaning of trust,
justification of my own existence,
there was no distance in the dark
when the fears fell away.

Forever for One Second

Forever for one second lingering,
dawn drinks night and lilac shadows slide,
silently slide, their glorious seconds ripe,
rays never were so near as now,
thoughts as mist slide around
expecting a miracle at dawn,
by touching shadows' silence they're kissed,
that we feel that we, like they, must live,
and nothing will fade away upon the afternoon,
we see, how gently rays cling, to that sound—
with that sound of heartbeat and expectation
as to the appearing morning city they sing,
our breath is with theirs forever loved.

Through Our Wishes

The wishes grow slowly in our minds,
but fast in our memories, and calm.
We all whisper or sing quietly,

second by second, word by word,
breath by breath,
saying "don't be afraid,"

saying "I love you,"
for the now is the point,
at which we all touch eternity.

Seconds—always starving lodgers of time,
took our thoughts away,
leaving the myriad small sparks

trying to shine a light through our wishes,
as the precious stone in dirt
cannot be consumed by slow decay,

not even dragged by force of doubt,
but strangely, right before dawn,
when you float on the edge of a night dream,

you hear a voice. It whispers in your ear,
and the light comes in, and the land appears,
but you are silent, frightened by the delayed seconds.

In your thoughts your childhood dives up,
you recall your parents,
the summertime,

when you caught locusts,
didn't know that your father's breath
would never leave you.

Your mother was young at that time,
her kind smile makes you cry now,
as if the smell of that summer has reached you.

The secret quietness the crickets' noise,
comes from a distance,
and the day passed so quickly,

you don't notice the twilight.
I miss your hands—
the velvet lights surrounding the vineyard at dawn.

I miss the smell of that velvet lights,
the smell of joy—
comforting through the centuries of dark,

and I miss your voice—
the sparkling water,
life-giving song of bone-dry past,

time passes as time does,
so much behind us—
thoughts without words,

when understanding means seeing,
and silence at dawn is the sound of kindness.
I want you to be the guiding word in silence,

calling me home.
Wake up, be the guiding word
in silence.

R Train

Subway car is almost empty.
R train / Brooklyn – Manhattan.
Woman in long black coat stands over there,

looking at her reflection on the car's door,
reflections of her smile are rushing away in the dark.
Why she smiles?

Maybe that kiss?
Maybe she guessed the meaning of her wish?
Maybe she can see whether her prayer is answered?

Train stopped at Canal Street.
Reflected upon its own reflection.
Door is open. She went out. She never looked back.

A Cloud

Days and nights— the division of grace.
I read the text message, today,
it was concerned with language,
and intonation. I tried to look out a window—
to see disappearing airplane
beyond that rooftop water tower.
One of the clouds resembled her face.
If you miss that cloud, it misses you as well.
If you see it, it sees you. That's the way of flight.
You will remember this present, and that cloud too,
that's the way of living.

A Wave

Through the labyrinths of glances,
as we flit between shadows,

memories curve over us like a wave.
Child sleeps. Mother put the machinegun down.

She knows not even the echo
of distant noise can touch child's breath,

the vision raised to the window
until the veins of night emerge

as air filled with loughs finally.
She sings lullaby, now, knowing

that the Lord found a time to listen
to her song.

By Our Presence

Smell of the grass, new cut, always follows the day,
when we expect the news. In our life,
we really look at each other once, in streets.
The rest is premonition or memory.
Walk in the street is a form of love,
we all are fascinated by our presence,
feeling that we will never meet each other again,
not knowing that we have whole life in common.

Chapter Three

The Structure of Central Ray

Empty Square

I feel sadness when I look at empty square,
or remember that time when I made my first wish.
Are the lessons really repeated until they are learned?

I'd go to that empty square,
we'd somehow be together in the end.
Are we really what we allow ourselves to be?

Divine Drunkenness

The wishes grow slowly in our minds,
but fast in our memories, and calm.
We are the grapes — time is the essence
of divine drunkenness, when truth emerges.

Sometimes the storms displace the world
without washing us away.
Here the mist is a single thought
floating within islands of silence,

but there is a problem in the world,
the problem of truth— don't you think
everything feels like a soulless copy
of something better you've already felt?

When prophets are around, we never confuse
the size of our prize with the size of our labor,
but we always do the same when prophets
disappear — we worship the golden calf.

We all whisper or sing quietly,
second by second, word by word,
breath by breath, for the now is the point,
at which we all touch eternity— drunk.

Statue of Liberty

Turquoise
shadows
of her
drift in the night,
she
who looks behind the sky,
and sees your wishes,
she
who glimpses inside the sky
and awakens.

Love Song of Rays

See the rays over there? Did you hear songs?
Yes, songs from the frontline? Mariupol.
The pearl encircled by rays.

Moscovites hate the rays, ray means freedom,
they don't understand freedom, they hate themselves,
that's why they hate the world, hiding faces in the dark.

"This is the end, beautiful friend," remember?
We need victory, over the spiritless corps,
not just a peace—

peace is a luxury, as this second is one more
deadly breath of time, we do not have much time
for peace, we have time only for victory.

Even shadows shake when mother's voice
echoes from far beyond. How can you say peace
should give you comfort? Peace does not dwell

on the other side of war, but victory.
Maybe there is no peace in the world,
that's why we should win.

See the voices of kids how colored the ground?

Each thing born from those rays is our hope.
Who can succeed with all those rays,

full of those voices? Rays blow through the blood.
Who would like to dictate to you?
Who among us is right? Most valuable?

Who most resembles God? Have you ever seen God?
Touch the rays in Mariupol and you will see.
If there is peace deep in the ground,

it should feel the fear and joy,
If there is peace it should be a memory,
but memory is not powerful enough,

is not beautiful at all, never forget we are free,
that's why we can see the rays.
We can smell the rays, touch them

with every beat of our hearts.
We are dying, we are living, not complaining,
we touched each other with our hearts

we were born in the hearts of each other,
we required life, because we all are in the war.
Touch the rays. Peace.

As the Breath of Mother

Silence is a spirit of word.
This night shadow drifts on the field as usual
sliding for a bit at the oak tree right in the center
of the night where it often sees itself surrounded
by the smells and fleeting glimpse to feel if it finds
any transfiguration.

My shadow looks at every leaf and the whole
body of a tree, it sees me, the same human being,
with the same heart—
the familiar outlines of life still clinging to it.
The oak tree seems, surrounded by night,
naked and close,

as the breath of mother, that's my outlines
drift again in the dark, it thinks—
everything in the dark is in some way a family
by faith. Shadows never slide alone,
turning that breath into a song.
Then dawn appears, on the edge of the field,

as the echo of silence, and the world is naked
at dawn, no one sees anymore how beautiful
that field was, but my shadow remembers, also,
that the oak tree embraced it, right here, slowly
drifting on the field watching the dark water
flashing on its velvet softness.

96-Year-Old Man

I was standing alone in front of the stillness
of March, not expecting the flow of memories.
We are living without love, that's why the war

can't be measured by history, by ashes, by art.
Without today we breathe between yesterday
and tomorrow. Do you know something about time?

About time, yes, and its insanity?
Do you know something about yourself?
About me? How've I lived? How've I loved?

What I did? Maybe you can predict future?
Time should have some meaning for you.
For me it's insanity.

I felt history's neurasthenia in that very afternoon
when I was standing in front of the stillness of March
and not expecting the flow of seconds. Nerves of time.

I understood and I did not expect to be alive,
time is meaningless and it's suppressing us.
I didn't expect to feel that deadly second again,

in emptiness, but my heart was able to beat again,

my heart is remembering, after centuries,
how to beat again in the frozen silence of fears,

war, in the raw,
cold breeze of the laughs
and howl.

96-year-old man.
Mr. Romanchenko.
Survived the concentration camps:
Buchenwald,
Peenemünde,
Mittelbau-Dora,
Bergen-Belsen.
Yesterday he was killed
by the Russian missile
hitting his apartment building in Kharkiv.

Russia, the "denazifier,"
did what the Nazis
couldn't do.

All the Shores of Mediterranean Sea

Twilight fades.
Beyond the shore a voice echoes.
I wasn't exactly when, but I realized,
it was dusk—
that chasm between, the crystal-pink
and the twin flame, the lilac flow—
all I knew was here and now,
when I fell in—
and all I could not
hope — a second that was
everything else other than our names,
an affinity, a breeze with sound, a cry of joy,
that tugs at our center of gravity.
Along the shores, the past rolls over us,
rushes by into the empty lanes where all our stories
are retold, where they carry on deep into the dark.
Are we the couple to whom that occurred?
What we thought we choose to become? I have all a man
might need but received much more. She kissed me, and said:
"Just drive, my love. There is something about the open road.
It makes our few footsteps feel like so many more."
Kissed by the wind like a sail, the galleon drives on.
I have been drowned and opened,
made whole and poignant by a wind
who casts me adrift.

Oh wind, we are made of quenching aspirations.
The passion of your sea lives within me,
and that kiss quenches me as a song—
as a song of time,
time passes as time does: so much behind us,
a little less to go. No easy ride: peace can be
vexing—what we've left behind as the sun
dips down low.

With a Million Smiles

With a million smiles and still lonely.
I said: "Only once. It's because we've forgotten our hearts."
You said: "Once is enough, if with compassion."
"Must have been a dream," I considered and said zero,
but late one night, on the knife-edge of dawn,
I found the words: "Once is enough," you mumbled,
your brow bracing the Mediterranean sky.
Looking at the flying triangle of storks up above,
I feel hope. Yet, we all are alone in our own journey,
but many are going with us, we do not know why,
we only know who the enemies of hope are,
leave them alone. Don't say a word.
I found a bridge in between us, when the footsteps will be yours,
and the echoes will be mine, maybe many rises up against us,
leave them alone, rewarding murdering psychopaths,
privileged parasites, will end up all together, don't look at them,
I found a garden for us, where the roses will be yours,
water will be mine, when the lips of ear, of course,
will kiss us time to time, when daylights never die,
when the smells of those rays will enrich all our nights.

Let It Sound

We hear a long familiar melody.
Let it sound as gratefulness of our breath.
Shadow falls from our eyes, my love.
Secrets always remain the same.
We do not hear the distant roar of gale, tonight.
We hear that melody; a tide that tugs at us.
The night is calm. Above our heads
a star will flame, again,
and we are not too old at all,
we glare at our night, and it is so clear
that there is never too late for a miracle,
when our eyes touch the night, our lips touch the words
as a secret language of our own breath addressing
a secret world, lifting our bodies to silky night's softness,
we realize how alive we are.

Remember Me

Standing on the edge of darkness, expecting
calmness, in the deadly noise and fury
of a century, do I not fear silence? Since I am
under the same sentence of condemnation?
And I indeed have been condemned justly,
for I am getting what I deserve for my deeds,
but silence has done nothing wrong,
I am looking up.
When I look at your naked beauty, dear air,
when I look at your strength, dear water,
when I look at your mercy, dear earth,
when I look at your holiness, dear fire,
I feel presence of all the languages
inside me, all around me, I feel they are the veins
of our world, where spirit of the world
is music itself, spirit of music is melody
itself, spirit of melody is harmony itself,
spirit of harmony is every sound of our
heartbeat,
as the world is breathing by silence only.
Oh, divine silence, remember me
when you come into your kingdom.

Empty Strollers in Front of You

See the empty strollers over there? In front of you.
Now you see what moskals are. Don't say a word.
Take a deep breath. Now you know what has happened,
why, how, where and when—
right here, not so far—
Not so far.
Just a second ago, they were alive.
My sweetest friend, they were loved.
The peace offering love—
Earth and heavens made sacrifices to that love,
the dews of their smiles are the words of holy.
Who ever heard or felt anything more divine?
Is there something precious we are longing to find out there?
Their voices hit your senses, burst your temples,
burn your breath. See the rays?
Or the black smoke under flawed stillness?
This is the other side of our happiness—
and its silence means the end.

Divine Ukraine

Your eyes are the eyes of God.
Your breath is mother tongue of Earth.
Your blood is a symphony of fire.
Your lips are the truth-tellers,
no one can take your golden mystery,
no one can feel you without admiration.
Your heart is garden of kisses.
Your ears are pearls of expectation.
Your words are constellations –
the faces of heroes, encircled by rays,
drifted on the minds of the world,
their smile, their look, their strength
and its innocence, a tide that tugs at us.
In times like these, a sense washes over us,
and we gather in the deadly noise of a millennium
and this stillness, a stillness that never wavers.
All we have become, divine Ukraine,
is what your innocence has made of us.
The naked homeland of freedom
beats right in your heart.

The Mirrors

I am not going to change you.
You are the mirror of myself.
As I am yours.
I still remember that bird
flying above Pearl Street
in the Financial District in Manhattan,
as if the sky was its mother,
the bird hugging and kissing the air,
the sky so close to me,
so clear, reflecting the buildings
on its transparent body
with centuries of revelations.
The sky was the mirror of earth,
that day, and I felt that smell,
the smell of expectation we both love.

Wolf Came to Me, Once

I thought about Faust.
"My perception creates my forest,"
said my guest. "My night and the moon.
What I look at doesn't matter,
but how I look at it does."
"I am not going to kill you,"
I spoke.
"How can I trust you?"
"I am a man of my word."
"Are you a poet?" Wolf stood near me.
"Who dominates on today's world of poetry?"

"Poetry does not dominate; it cultivates,"
I hear in my mind and wolf said:
"Today's world is a world of mysteries,
you better run, you better fly."

If I Speak in the Tongues of Men

"If I speak in the tongues of men and of angels,
but have not love, I am only a resounding gong
or a clanging cymbal. If I have the gift of prophecy
and can fathom all mysteries and all knowledge,
and if I have a faith that can move mountains,
but have not love, I am nothing."

–1 Corinthians 13:1

*

There is no time to be lost. Who can lose by giving?
No one. Never. Who can lose by holding back?
Everyone. Always. We have paid the cost.
We breathe in between yesterday and tomorrow.
We know how to win without boasting
or lose without excuse. Peace cannot be waxing
it helps to take a deeper breath.

I saw you standing quietly under the balcony, that night.
214 Bay 14th Street. Brooklyn, New York.
I called your name. Our heartbeat echoes burned
the street, a stillness broken before dawn,
in the name of all that is hailed, in the name of
our very present, in the face of it all—

the remaining past unclaimed, driven forth by love.
Waiting for a miracle—
we are speechless, but we know language of silence,
spinning chaos into order, looking for an exit—
trying to recall a memory of us in the great affliction
of time. Our past seconds are our roots.
All the constellations are our eyes.

Our seeds are our thoughts, listening to your voice
on the other side of silence gives me the courage to lose
sight and swim there, your voice is hope trusting the flow,
it calls me now: we are what we hear, doubt is deadlier,
but fear cuts deeper than air, and we are not moving toward
revenge, we forgive the world its own loneliness,

but I have good news – we will all get out of here alive.
What happens, happens on time, don't seek your fault.
Nothing is your fault. There is no fault at all, but living,
through the mysteries of forgiving.

I see we are waiting for a miracle, the miracles happen
when I trust you, my sweetest friend, but nothing happens
when I cannot talk with you, and cannot keep my faith,
when I cannot continue my path when no one is around me,
when I cannot trust myself when all men doubt me.

Distance means nothing when your loved one means everything
and I am telling you – we will all get out of here alive.

What does not happen, does not happen in time, don't seek
your or others' fate. There is no fate at all, but choice,
in the centuries of noise and its deadly drive, while I am
telling you – we will all get out of here alive.

Acknowledgments

I would like to thank the publisher for selecting this work for publication and believing in my message and story I must tell.

Thank you to those who wrote testimonials for my book: Aaron Fischer, DW Gibson, Thelma T. Reyna, Wayne Miller, Judy Turek, Linda Galbraith, Lucas Hirsh, McKenzie Lynn Tozan.

I would like to thank our friends and family for believing in me and for appreciating and respecting the time and effort it took away from them to create and revise this work.

I'd also like to give special thanks to Irakli Gabriel, who was more than generous with his expertise and precious time.

Credits

"Heaven Hear Us" – previously appeared in
    Braided Way Magazine. USA, 2024

"Streets" – previously appeared in Stanford
    University Poetry Lab / Spilwords Press, The
    Writers and Readers' Magazine, the world
    edition of Quarantine Stories Magazine,
    Poetry Festival Magazine, performed by the
    actress Allison Kampf for the same festival
    and anthologized by Thelma T. Reyna,
    Golden Foothills Press of the American
    Anthology of Pandemic Poetry. USA, 2020.

Also, this poem was featured on the huge posters
    in the streets of Wellington, New Zealand,
    2022.

"The Heart of the Cyclone" / "Before Dawn" –
    previously appeared in Anthologized by
    Thelma T. Reyna Golden Foothills Press of
    the American Anthology of Pandemic Poetry.
    USA, 2020.

"Hope" – previously appeared in Spectrum
    Publishing. USA, 2020.

"For a Second" – previously appeared in Vita
    Brevis Magazine. Named as an Editor's
    Choice. USA 2018

"A Bird Above New York City" A winning poem of Adelaide Book Poetry Anthology in a category of Best Poem 2020. Previously appeared in Amethyst Review. USA, 2020.

"D Train" – previously appeared in Poetry Superhighway Magazine, as a Publication of Week. USA, 2022, and in Highland Park Poetry. USA, 2024.

"A Few Centuries Pass" – previously appeared in California Poppy Times Magazine. USA, 2023.

"Take Your Sandals of Your Feet" – previously appeared in OpenDoor Poetry Magazine. USA, 2022.

"If I Speak in the Tongues of Men / I Have Good News" – previously appeared in Poetry Media lab by the Stanford University, The Visible Magazine. USA, 2020

"Divine Ukraine" – previously appeared in OpenDoor Poetry Magazine, Organized Chaos Magazine, Wildfire Words. USA / UK 2020 Journal. USA / Turkey, 2020

"Empty Strollers in Front of You" – previously appeared in Organized Chaos magazine. USA, 2020

"Forever for One Second" – previously appeared in The Scene Magazine. USA, 2023.

"Fog" – previously appeared in South Broadway Press. USA, 2023.

"Wolf Came to Me Once" – previously appeared in The Visible Magazine. USA, 2021

"Through Our Wishes" – previously appeared in Lit Shark Magazine. USA, 2024

"The Flow of the Current" – previously appeared in Platform Review / Arts by the People. USA, 2024

"The Sky Is Clear Tonight" – previously appeared in Platform Review / Arts by the People. USA, 2024

"Jerusalem" – previously appeared in Live Encounters Magazine and in Amethyst Review. USA / UK, 2024

"As the Breath of Mother" – previously appeared in Cultural Daily. USA, 2023

"Forest" – previously appeared in Litehouse. Portugal, 2020

"Love Song of Rays" – previously appeared in The BeZine Journal, USA, 2022

"96-Year-Old Man" – previously appeared in The BeZine Journal. USA, 2022

"All the Shores of Mediterranean Sea" – previously appeared in Mediterranean Poetry Magazine. Sweden, 2021

"Let It Sound" – previously appeared in Life and Legends Magazine. USA, 2021

"Remember Me" – previously appeared in Life and Legends Magazine. USA, 2021

"With a Million Smiles" – previously appeared in Mediterranean Poetry Magazine. Sweden, 2021

"The Mirrors" – previously appeared in Lehrhaus. USA, 2024

"Divine Drunkenness" – previously appeared in Poetry Potion Magazine. USA, 2024

"Statue of Liberty" – previously appeared in Highland Park Poetry. USA, 2024

"A Cloud" – previously appeared in Feral: A Journal of Poetry and Art. USA, 2024

DAVID DEPHY (he/him) (pronounced as "DAY-vid DE-fee") is an American award-winning poet and novelist. The founder of Poetry Orchestra. Poet-in-Residence for Brownstone Poets 2024. His poem, "A Sense of Purpose," is going to the Moon by The Lunar Codex, NASA, and Brick Street Poetry in 2024. He was exiled from his native country of Georgia in 2017 and was granted political asylum in the USA immediately and indefinitely. His family, beloved wife and 9-year-old son joined him in the U.S. after 7 years of exile in 2023. He lives and works in New York City.